Invisible Mothers

when love doesn't die

By Emily R. Long, LPC

Printed in the United States of America
First Printing 2015
ISBN 978-0-9965556-0-9

Firefly Grace Publishing
292 Woody Lane Suite A
Asheville, NC 28804
www.EmilyRLong.com

Interior Design: ShiftFWD
Cover Design: Davon Embler

For Grace and Lily
Always.

Also,
For the daughter of my Aunt Suz,
born still August 22, 1974

For the son of my Grandma Long,
David Allen
1/24/49 - 1/25/49

For all the mothers aching in the silence for their children to hold,
You are not alone.

Contents

Gratitude & Love

To Mom and Dad: You have always loved, supported, and encouraged me along my crazy path. You gave me a foundation of unconditional love and the wings to fly. I love you.

To my chosen family: You beamed a light that brought me home to myself. You brighten my life every day. I love you.

To Amy Davis: Without your absolute faith, kick-my-ass coaching, and incredible love this book may not have come to be. You truly are a burst of love and sunlight in my life. I love you.

To Barbara Waterhouse: You were the first to hear Grace's name and the first to call me a mother. Thank you for being my teacher. I love you.

To Amy Hermodson: You taught me a great deal in the classroom. You taught me so much more about the beauty of learning to live while grieving. Those hours in your office were like a balm to a very raw and wounded heart. I will always remember your Anna. I love you.

To all the mothers who entrusted me with your stories and children for this book: You are my inspiration. You were held close with every word I wrote. You made this book possible.

To my editors: You made this book better, clearer, and more beautiful. Thank you for bringing your gifts to this project.

And to Grace & Lily: This is for you. Thank you for being my children and my teachers. There is nothing I cannot do because I am your mother. Mama loves you, always.

Also, extra thanks to my favorite local coffee shops: City Bakery (Charlotte Street) and Edna's of Asheville as well as All Good Coffee of Weaverville for supplying bagels and the many cups of hot cocoa that fueled the writing of this book :)

Breaking the Silence

It was my daughter's would-have-been 6th birthday when I realized that no one had ever spoken her name to me and, other than me, no one remembered that she had lived.

It was then that I finally told someone about her life, and her death. It was the first time I'd spoken of her to anyone. I cried for the pain of her loss and the freedom of being seen and heard for the first time. Finally, the pain and grief that had pressed so heavily around my heart for so many years began to ease just the slightest bit.

That moment of realization, and of finding my voice, was the initial seed of this book coming to life.

As the years have passed since that day, I have talked of my Grace and her younger sister, Lily, with many. I speak openly of their lives, their deaths and my grief process. Remembering and acknowledging them eases the terrible ache of not being able to hold them, nurture them, and mother them the way I want to in this lifetime. The more I talk of them, the more alive they feel to me.

When I am able to talk of them and acknowledge their lives, I feel less like an invisible mother and am simply their mother.

In the twelve years since my first daughter's stillbirth, I have looked for books about mothers like me. I found countless books on pregnancy loss and child loss in general. I found many books on pregnancy after loss and parenting after loss.

I found nothing on what it is to be a mother without any living children. I could find nothing on what it is to heal from loss without either having a living child born before loss or a living child born after loss.

It felt like there was no one else like me. When the isolation and loneliness of my grief felt unbearable, there was nothing I could reach for to remind me that I wasn't alone. If there were others like me, it seemed no one was talking about it. Even in baby loss communities, this experience of being a mother without living children wasn't really being acknowledged.

That is, in part, what this book is about. It is about giving other mothers like me, mothers who have lost their babies and who don't have any other living children, the acknowledgment they rarely receive. I want this book to be there, available in those dark moments of isolation and loneliness to let other mothers know, "I see you. I know that you love. I see your motherhood. You are not alone."

I did eventually realize that I wasn't alone in this experience of mothering without a physical child here. When I first started the process of this book, I still wasn't entirely sure that I wasn't alone. As I reached out and started talking I discovered that there are many invisible mothers in the world. So many of these mothers are also searching for someone who shares their experience. Finding them helped pieced together a crack in my heart.

This book is not a dry, academic book on grief or child loss. It's both personal and professional – and more. For this book project, nearly 50 other invisible mothers came forward to share their stories and their experiences with me. They are a small group among the thousands of invisible mothers who live in our world.

These mothers come from all across the United States as well as five other countries. They come from a wide variety of backgrounds with diverse faith systems, sexual orientation, relationship status, professions, cultures, family structures, loss experiences, political backgrounds, and more. Their ages range from 20 to 65.

The experience of loss also varies widely among these amazing mothers. There are differences in how the loss occurred, how they thought about it, the support they received, what they wanted for support and much more.

Yet despite wide variations in backgrounds, ages, and experiences, there are also remarkably similar experiences among these mothers regarding their grief, their longing for their children, the aching emptiness, the desire to talk about their experience and love for their children. There are far too many similarities to be ignored.

This book is about giving a voice to those without any living children – the ones often unseen as mothers by society, the world and even their families. It's about acknowledging the mothers who don't have a physical child people can point to and say, "Yes, she's a mother."

Not everyone will agree with what I write in this book. Even some of the mothers I interviewed will find pieces that don't fit for them. That's okay. I encourage everyone to take what you find beneficial and useful from this book and to simply leave what doesn't fit for you. I am adamant about the fact that there is not one right way to grieve – there is only your way.

Feel free to disagree with me and to have a different perspective. The second reason for this book is simply to start conversations around these topics. Grief. Miscarriage. Stillbirth. Infant and child death. I want our world to stop being afraid to talk about these things. Babies and children die. Grief happens. Remaining silent and pretending it doesn't happen isn't serving anyone or anything but the promotion of our own discomfort.

Grief and loss affects each of us differently. We all grieve and heal in our own unique ways and on our own individual timelines. There are no rules to grief or healing. I have always been adamant about the fact that there is no wrong way to grieve or heal.

However, I will make one exception to my stance on that. Silent grief festers. Grieving in silence and isolation hinders our ability to love and live and find the beauty in life again.

No one deserves to grieve in silence and isolation. Our discomfort with death and grief isn't a good enough reason to keep quiet. Keeping quiet only leads to shame, isolation, and more pain for those experiencing the death of their baby or child. Remaining silent only perpetuates fear and shame.

Or as Paula so succinctly put it, "*We need to talk about the unspeakable because the unspeakable happens.*"

Have conversations. Talk with people going through this experience. Ask them what their experience is like and how you can be there for them. Disagree with me and tell me about it. Ask other people what they think. Acknowledge that these painful circumstances still happen in the world. Move through the fear. Bring light to the shame, isolation, and pain. Become comfortable with the uncomfortable.

Speak out and speak up. Let's break the silence together.

Part One:

Our Experience of Love & Loss

love

A Mother's Love

The moment that I realized I was pregnant with my daughter Grace is one of the clearest and most joy-filled memories that I have. I can close my eyes twelve years later and recall that moment in utter clarity. Even then, in the shock and disbelief of her unplanned arrival, this pull of love was so strong and intense I knew there was nothing I would not do to keep her safe. In that instant, life changed. I was a mother.

What matters most about my experience as a mother without living children is not about the loss of my children. It's about how deeply I love them. It's that they lived. It's about how they made me a mother and how fundamentally they changed who I am.

I am not alone in that. What came out again and again in my interviews for this book was how much our babies are loved and valued. We love them beyond words, beyond death, through immense pain and grief, and for the rest of our living life. Our grief is big, deep, and powerful because our love is equally big, deep, and powerful. Our babies' tiny bodies might have faded away, but our mother love never dies.

Many mothers talked about this intense, gripping love that appeared with the first line of the pregnancy test or the words from the doctor confirming they were pregnant. For some it was the first moment they suspected they might be pregnant. Others talked about feeling this love long before their baby's life took hold in their body – love that came from waiting and preparing through years of trying to get pregnant both naturally or through fertility treatments. For them, it was a love that only intensified exponentially with that first positive pregnancy test.

One mother described her joy in finding out she was pregnant, *"We'd waited a long time to have a baby. When I found out I was finally pregnant, I was so excited I could hardly stand it. I wanted to tell everyone I saw that I was carrying my precious baby and I was finally a mommy."*

Lisa stated that when she finally got pregnant after 7 years, *"It felt unbelievable that we were pregnant. We loved him so much right away and felt as if he was the baby we were meant to have."*

Is it the same love that comes when a mother gets to hold her living child in her arms for the first time? I don't know. I've never experienced that. I can say that being able to hold my daughter Grace's body simply made me all the more aware of the love I had for her and what I had hoped for her life. There was overwhelming love and shattering grief in equal measure. My love for her has not only remained deep and powerful, but has grown immensely in the many years since her life and death.

One of the common sayings one hears spoken by mothers is, "You don't know real love until you hold your child in your arms." Sometimes when I hear that, the small part of me that remains bitter about the death of my daughters wants to respond with, "No, you don't know real love until you *can't* hold your children in your arms."

The question, however, isn't about whose love is more real, but rather, why do we feel the need to evaluate love? Why do we feel the need to compare our love? Why can't we simply love our children and honor our experiences of love and motherhood? We are all mothers who love our children.

The tiny bodies of our babies might fade away, but the love and value and gift of their life lives on, burning brightly within us forever.

One mother talked about wanting people to understand that although our children's lives were so brief, their lives still count and their lives make an impact on the world. She talked about only having her son for the nine months of her pregnancy and although they knew that he would not survive, they valued and cherished the time they did have with him. He had an incredible impact, not just on her and her partner's life, but also on the lives of their family and friends. His brief time here on earth touched many lives.

Lisa stated, *"They are our children forever – alive or dead. My life on the outside hasn't changed much day-to-day because I don't have a child here to care for. But inside, I am changed forever. "*

It's true, on the surface it often appears as if nothing has changed in our lives. I suspect this is part of why it's so hard for people to understand the depth of our loss and the change that occurs in us when our babies die. Others can't always see the magnitude of the change that happens in us with our babies' lives, and then their deaths.

Lisa put it like this, *"We expect life to be different when we are expecting our child, but when they die, after the initial upheaval and shock, our lives go back to their former day-to-day. The changes we were prepared to make suddenly aren't there."*

One of the most challenging aspects of losing our babies is when people ignore the fact that they lived. It cuts deep and wide to have people brush off the value of their lives with statements such as "you'll have more, you are young yet" as if they could simply be replaced by another baby. Or the even more painful, "It was only a fetus, not even a baby yet" that dismisses the life of our baby completely.

We go on with our day-to-day activities of work, household routines, and social responsibilities. Everything looks the same from the outside. The changes we expected to make to bring a child into our lives to love and raise didn't happen. Once the initial chaos and shock of our baby's death has passed, our lives often go back to the former day-to-day routine.

Except nothing is the same. We aren't the same people. This love we have for our children changes us – just as it changes those mothers whose children live.

Jennifer shared that people around her often acted "as if the last year and a half just didn't happen." She stated that it was as if the nine months of her pregnancy as well as the initial grief-filled months after her daughter's stillbirth simply disappeared in the eyes of those around her. What came instead was an assumption that life was simply going on as it always had.

"It's like my daughter never existed. Very few ever mention her by name or talk with me about her or ask about how I'm doing. It's as if she's an invisible child and I'm an invisible mother. I'm haunted by the what if's of my daughter's life and few want to even acknowledge she was here."

It has been more than a decade since my daughter Grace was born still and I still love her every bit as much as I did while she lived inside me. I will love her until I leave this earth.   And, although I had a briefer and different relationship with her sister Lily, who died at 10 weeks of pregnancy, I love her every bit as much as I love Grace.

It's common, unfortunately, to hear comparing of losses within the pregnancy and baby loss communities as well as the larger societal community. An assumption is often made that it is less painful to lose a baby early in pregnancy. People often assume that there is less of a relationship and less time for love for the baby to grow if the baby dies early.

Now, it is possible that some mothers aren't as bonded or attached to their children until later in pregnancy or after birth. Not every mother easily and quickly bonds with her baby, and that can be a source of pain and loss in and of itself.

However, to assume that someone experiences less love or less grief when her child dies early in pregnancy, or early in life for that matter, is mistaken. Time is but a single factor among dozens that contribute to the experience of love and loss. Many mothers try for years for that positive pregnancy test. When the moment finally comes they can see their child's entire life spread out before them. Others, like myself, are surprised and scared when the test comes back positive, yet are filled with this rush of awe and love bigger than anything we have ever experienced.

I was struck by comments that one of the mothers I interviewed made regarding her relationship with her son who died at 11 weeks of pregnancy. She talked about how she thought about her baby on some level every minute of her pregnancy and in those weeks she built a beautiful, loving relationship with him.

"From the moment I knew, I became We and I was never alone. I interacted daily with my baby – talked with him, sang to him, thought about what food I was eating for him. Everything I was doing was because of him."

Her time with her son here in the physical world was brief, yet filled with more connection and greater depth than some ever experience in their lifetime. The age of the baby or the length of the pregnancy has no ability to predict the level of impact of the loss.

Depth of love has no basis in time.

My Sweet Grace,

I am so proud to be your mother. I am grateful, always, that you choose me to be your mama and to carry you in this life. Your life made my life better. Because of you I love deeper, live more fully, and see more of the beauty of life. I carried your body for such a brief time, but I will carry your spirit with me forever.

Letting you go was the hardest thing I have ever had to do. Every day I have to let go of the girl that you might have been. I miss you beyond measure. I miss who you were and who you might be if you were here with me.

The hope of you, the joy of knowing you were with me, carried me through the grief and desperate sorrow after your father died. You taught me that no matter how deep the darkness, there was always beauty to be found. Although the tiny body in which your spirit lived faded away, the beauty that is you will live on in me for all my days.

Thank you, sweet girl, for gifting me with your life and for being my greatest teacher.

Mama loves you, always.

xoxo,
Mama

Depth of love has no basis in time

loss

Unimaginable Loss

Losing our babies shifts the entire foundation of our lives. What once felt solid and steady suddenly moves under us, uprooting everything we thought we knew about life. The entire landscape of our live is changed in an instant when a tsunami of grief and pain sweeps away all that was familiar.

Let me be blunt. Unless you've experienced the loss of your only child(ren), you cannot understand the depth and the magnitude of this loss that we live with every day. Even those who have lost a child but have other living children cannot fully understand this kind of loss. Nothing that I write in this book will really be able to give you a true understanding of it. Trying to help you to comprehend what we experience isn't really the point of this book. Raeanne put it beautifully by saying,

"As a woman, I can't know what it's like to be a man. But that doesn't mean I can't listen to their experience and trust that their experience is as they describe. I can be open-hearted and listen to their truth."

It's not my desire to try to convince you of the long-lasting depth of this loss. It's my desire to offer chance for myself and other mothers like me to have their voices heard and to share their experience. It's a chance for you to hear our experience and gain a new perspective.

The truth is, our loved ones don't have to fully understand our experience as invisible mothers. Understanding is not a requirement for offering support, love, and kindness. What I hope people will gain from this book is a realization of how valuable and important your love and support is to us, even if you don't understand our experience.

One of the more painful pieces of learning to live through this kind of loss is how quickly support can drop off. Too often, just weeks or months after the death of our children, people around us are expecting us to have "moved on" and to "be back to normal." I'm not sure the pain of this loss really lessens over time as is commonly told to those of us who experience it. Perhaps the sharp edges of it smooth out a bit and round over, but what I believe is that those of us who carry it become stronger. I believe that the longer we carry the heaviness of this pain and loss, the stronger our mental and emotional muscle becomes. Over time, as our muscle gets stronger, the weight of our loss becomes easier to carry. The loss doesn't change, we change. Another way to describe it is to imagine a tree that has had a thick nail driven into it. The nail never goes away nor does it get smaller. It remains forever, piercing into the tree's very being. The tree, however, adapts to the nail and grows around it, making the nail part of itself. Our loss, like the nail, never goes away. We simply take it into us and grow around, over, and with it. Our loss becomes part of who we are. We walk with this loss every day, carry it with us to work, to gatherings with friends and family, in all our activities, when we laugh and cry and in every moment we live.

The wounds of this loss don't fade away with time despite our world's often touted "time heals all wounds" mentality. No, the wound doesn't disappear. But we humans are resilient beings and we learn to live with this wound. We grow scar tissue to cover it and we adapt to make it part of our being. Perhaps it is a form of healing as it becomes part of who we are and we do move forward with living. It isn't, however, a passive process and it does leave a permanent mark. Over time, with growth and evolution, our loss becomes integrated into who we are. It influences our choices, our perception of life, our sense of self, and plays a role in shaping who we become.

However, although we grow stronger and more resilient with this loss, this doesn't mean that the support and kindness of loved ones isn't still necessary and valuable. The tree may grow to integrate the nail that pierced it, but the tree still needs water and soil and sunshine in order to live and thrive. In the same way, we still need love, kindness, and support as we move forward in life.

Dear Ander,

I want to tell you about all the amazing things you got to do before you were born. You were at the engagement dinner for Aunt M and Uncle E, where we ate butternut squash ravioli; you went to a Cubs game with K and J and their baby-to-be. You went camping, and when you were just a little tadpole, you learned how to whitewater canoe with your mommies. You did a lot of traveling, though I don't think you liked flying much, and you really didn't like the trains. You listened to opera at Italian Fest; you walked with us on the beach at Kohler-Andre State Park on a beautiful, hot day and boogied (gently) at the Dancing Festival in Millennium Park (mostly, you liked watching other people dance).

Your mommy believes that the night before you died, you gave us a gift. On Thursday, we held you, and your oxygen saturation went from the 60s to the 80s. We hoped that, like the night before you first coded, you would stay there for a while, maybe for good this time. With you so stable, we got some solid sleep for the first time in several nights. Thank you for that gift, for hitting the 80s for your mamas so that we could rest physically and emotionally in preparation for Friday, which we now know was your last day with us. Thank you, baby, for that gift of sleep.

We never got to hear you cry, but I cherished the little "squeaks" that were caused by air leaks around your ventilator tube. I hope it wasn't you crying;

you didn't otherwise seem upset. In fact, they were often evident when we were holding you, when you would push your little feet against my belly to nuzzle up closer to my heart and my chin. I would drop my head to nuzzle my chin against your downy head; the best feeling in the world.

It's still hard to feel like your mama, since we never really got to mother you. But we did, a bit. We changed your diapers, took your temperature, wiped your nose and eyes and mouth, fed you colostrum swabs, and cuddled and loved you for days. We sang to you and told you how proud we were of you, and we felt the most powerful love that I still don't believe could ever be replicated. We so, so wish we could have kept you longer.

We love you, baby boy.

Mama

Understanding is not a requirement for offering support, love, and kindness.

isolation,
silence &
shame

Shining a Light on Isolation, Silence, and Shame

One of the other aspects of our loss that can be difficult for those around us to grasp is the impact that it has on our sense of identity. Few people talk about the profound identity crisis that can occur with loss of this nature. Having your only child(ren) die or struggling with infertility can leave one floundering in a sea of questions and uncertainty such as:

Who am I without my child?

Who am I if I don't ever have children to raise?

Who am I when my former happy, optimistic, care-free self seems to have disappeared?

Who is the person who can't stop crying and is overwhelmed with anger and grief?

Who am I as a woman if my body can't do what's "natural" and conceive or give birth to a living baby?

There is often a lot of talk about "returning to normal" after loss. We long for life to feel familiar again and desperately desire to be our old selves. Friends and family tell us that they miss who we were and they wish things would "get back to normal." Unfortunately, that normal doesn't exist anymore. This loss fundamentally changes us in irreversible ways. Our former self dies along with our babies and we cannot be the women we were again.

Instead, we have to create a new sense of normal. We have to create a new sense of identity and make sense of who we are now. We have to rediscover ourselves, as do the people who love us. This can be a painful and confusing process for everyone. It generally takes far, far longer than any of us expect or want.

However much our loved ones might miss us, we miss ourselves even more. It is a lonely place to be, that space where you no longer know yourself and those around you don't recognize you either. We aren't who we once were and we aren't yet who we will be. We need time to navigate the gap in our sense of self.

We'll probably need more time than you'd wish to give us.

What happens when we are pressured to move on faster is more isolation and shame. One of the things I hear the most from mothers working to find their way through this bewildering grief is how lonely the journey often feels. When I started using the phrase "invisible mothers" I got repeated messages from mothers saying, "Yes! That's it. That's how I feel."

Over and over I hear these words being used to describe the experience of being a mother without living children:

Invisible.

Isolated.

Alone.

Unseen.

Unheard.

Forgotten.

Unloved.

The sense that our children are forgotten and our motherhood is invisible can be pervasive and painful. For many of us, few people speak our children's names. Family members often exclude them from the list of grandchildren or nieces and nephews. After the first year, our children's birthdays often go unnoticed, or unmentioned, by anyone other than us. Mother's Day is often a day that passes without recognition or acknowledgement that we, too, are mothers though our children are no longer here in the physical world.

Beyond the invisibility and isolation of this experience, criticism and judgment is frequently thrown at us should we attempt to express our grief or the hurt of this invisibility and silence. This criticism and judgment comes in the form of hurtful statements such as:

"I thought you were over this now."

"Why can't you just let this go?"

"It's not healthy to hold onto this. Isn't it time you stopped wallowing in it?"

"You were only X weeks along, why are you making such a big deal out of this?"

"You aren't any fun anymore. Stop bringing everyone down."

"I wish you'd stop whining about this and get over it."

"You just need to focus on the gift in this and be positive."

I could go on with dozens of variations of these kinds of statements. Let's be clear about what is being said in these statements. First, the "this" so many people state is a baby who died. Second, I think what is forgotten about this kind of loss is that it isn't a singular, one-time event. I suspect people think of it as such: an event that happens at a moment in time and is done. Over. Complete. Perhaps for them, it is.

But for us, for those of who experience the death of our children, it isn't just a moment in time that finishes and is complete. This is an experience that we live with for the rest of our lives. There is no end point to it. It changes and evolves and morphs into different forms, but it does not end. The death of our baby is simply the beginning of this lifelong process of learning to live without our children and with this grief.

Hurt and feelings of rejection, isolation, abandonment, shame, and of being judged are strong in baby loss communities. Friends and family who often have good intentions or simply don't understand the loss feel hurt and confused when their actions or words are met with anger and withdrawal.

Mothers feel hurt, abandoned, and rejected by the actions or non-actions of their family and friends. Statements of criticism and judgment such as those above increase feelings of shame, guilt, and isolation. Too often when mothers hear statements such as those, they close down and silence themselves, putting on a mask of "I'm fine" while grief and pain continue to run rampant within them.

I can't tell you how many times I stayed silent when the grief felt overwhelming or said, "I'm fine," when I wasn't, because I didn't want to make my family or friends feel uncomfortable or didn't want to be Debbie Downer. Other times, I stayed silent out of fear that if I did try to talk about it, I would be met with impatience or criticism and be told to "move on" and "get over it" as has happened countless times. So the pain festered silently and contributed to years of depression and misery. I now know I'm not alone in that. During the interviews for this book, I repeatedly heard similar stories.

Anne shared that she struggled to know how to ask for support because "I don't want to make them feel bad."

Rachelle talked about feeling obligated to "tone down" her grief for others because they didn't want to talk about it.

Lisa shared that she has found blogging to be an easier outlet for talking about her loss because she often feels like people think she's "harping on about it" and wish she would stop.

Statements telling us to move on, get over it, and other similar judgments not only lead to feelings of silence and isolation, they can also amplify feelings of guilt, shame, and brokenness. There is frequently a great deal of pressure, from within us and from those around us, to get over our grief faster, to move on quicker, and to forget. When we can't, we feel as if there is something wrong with us. Even when we know intellectually that this loss is something we will experience for a lifetime, doubts and feelings of wrongness can plague us. As you may expect, that doesn't make this experience any easier to live through.

We don't like being in this place of grief and sorrow anymore than you like to see us here. No one wants to be able to move past this experience more than we do. And with time, probably longer than our loved ones would wish, we do eventually move through and return to living a full life again. However, chances are, we may have very different views on what moving on means.

I suspect what those who haven't experienced this kind of loss mean by the phrase "moving on" is to stop talking about it, forget, and return to normal. This isn't what moving on really means. Moving on is about learning to live again while grieving. It's about integrating the loss of our babies into in who we are and how we live while creating a beautiful, fulfilling life without them.

It has been twelve years since my daughter Grace died. I still miss her every day. I still look for her in all the children I see. I ache to hold her and hear her laugh. Holidays are filled with emptiness and longing that cannot be filled. I mark every would-have-been developmental milestone in my head, wondering who she would be and what it would be to mother her in this physical world. I light a candle on a cupcake every year on her birthday and celebrate the life that was. I may very well do these things until the day I leave this earth myself.

It does not, however, mean I am consumed by grief, broken by this loss, or somehow pathological in my grief because I continue to miss her and Lily. I am happy and ambitious and fiery and successful. My life is rich and full and beautiful. It is filled with the brilliance of my love for them and the shadows of their loss. Moving on does not equal forgetting. I am living while grieving. There is nothing healthier or more beautiful than that. That is what moving on actually looks like. This is true for all mothers like me.

Too often, as a counselor, I have heard clients talk about how family members or friends are concerned about their continued desire to talk about, remember, and honor their children even after many years. People often want us to just move on already and stop all this uncomfortable talk of dead babies. Our society, unfortunately, has a tendency to want to brush grief and death under the rug within days and never speak of it again.

Countless parents continue to honor and recognize their babies at birthdays and holidays for many years. Pictures and ultrasound images are kept on the wall. Gravestones are tended, decorated, and visited regularly even after many years. Special boxes with mementos or alters are kept in the home to honor and recognize their children's lives. Tears are shed as milestone after milestone that should have been pass with no child to experience them. All of this is especially true for those of us who never have living children.

This is normal.

It makes me cringe, both personally and professionally, to see grief become pathologized. The fact that a grieving mother can be diagnosed with clinical depression after just two weeks breaks my heart and makes me angry. Grief is not abnormal. Continuing to engage in these normal acts of remembrance does not mean we are "stuck" in our grief or that we are clinically depressed. These acts of honoring and remembering are simply our way of mothering a child that we can no longer hold.

The love and loss of our children will be with us for the rest of our lives. The ways in which we remember and celebrate their lives are symbols of our strength, motherhood, and, in fact, our emotional health.

Learning to find the beauty of living and embracing the fullness of life again after the loss of our children is quite possibly the most challenging process any of us may have to face. Doing it without the love and support of those around us makes it infinitely more difficult and typically prolongs the process. We are doing the best we can at any given moment. This isn't an experience that can be fixed. No words or actions on anyone's part can bring our babies back or take our grief away. But you can help lift those feelings of isolation and silence by simply being with us, loving us where we are and giving us the space to talk about whatever we are going through in that moment.

Dear Samuel,

Mama loves you with all her heart. When I think back on our time together, my heart is torn between the overwhelming joy of your life, and the devastating anguish of your absence. For every moment of happiness reliving your life, there's always a twinge of longing and sadness following closely behind. Both are my constant reality. More than anything, I'm incredibly proud of you and your life. You will always be my little warrior. I cherish you and our months together. When I feel like I can't go on, I think of your sweet face, your soft hair, brown eyes, and big boy hands and feet. Somehow, within those memories, I find the strength to continue facing each day. I know that if you could survive for as long as you did, despite all the obstacles you faced, then I can find a way to survive too.

Every day I miss you, and every day I long to see you grow. Our house never feels like a home, because your room is always empty, the silence always deafening. There are times when I can almost imagine you still here. The big boy you'd be now. The way you'd talk and laugh and play. It seems like I may never be happy again without you, but I'll try to be brave for you.

Thank you for making me a mother, and changing me to my core. Despite the terrible outcome, I'd chose you again, every time. Always remember, my little love, that you were wanted. You are loved. You are missed. Though death has stolen you from my arms, nothing can take you from my heart.

You are my special little guy, forever.

Love and kisses, Mama

*The love and loss of our children will
be with us for the rest of our lives.
The ways in which we remember and
celebrate their lives are symbols of our
strength, motherhood, and, in fact,
our emotional health.*

emotional storm

The Emotional Storm

As nice as it might be, there is not a roadmap or rulebook for how to live through grief. It's different for each of us. Grief is complex and multifaceted. Grief has no normal. Sorrow and sadness are just the leading edge of the emotional storm that comes after the death of our babies.

Much more than simple sorrow, there is a storm of anger and guilt, jealousy and envy, shame and blame that pervades lives, disrupts relationships, and drowns our sense of security in the world. It is a storm that rages out of nowhere, knocking us off our feet and turning life upside down.

When I was in high school, a tornado ripped through my grandparents' neighborhood, leveling houses and trees and buildings in mere seconds. Their house sustained some damage, but was structurally sound and standing. Directly across the street, four blocks wide and a mile long, were only piles of rubble and debris.

When my oldest daughter died, I remember thinking of that tornado and about the first time trying to drive to my grandparents' house afterward. After the tornado tore through, and even after the clean-up efforts and rebuilding, finding their house was confusing. For several years, I remember feeling lost and uncertain of my way because all the familiar landmarks that pointed the route to their house were gone. The houses and parks and landscapes that I had always used to guide my route had been demolished and cleared away.

Life after the death of our babies is remarkably similar to that confusing, unmarked, and unfamiliar post-tornado drive.

Much of the grief and sorrow we experience after the death of our babies is centered on the loss of them, of their life, and of our life with them. Some of what we are experiencing, however, is also grief and sadness over the loss of our sense of identity, our worldview, and ourselves. We also often grieve the change in relationships with those we love. Many parents who experience the death of their baby also experience a loss of close relationships with friends and family. People who were once a frequent part of our lives suddenly disappear without warning or leave out of frustration that we aren't who we used to be. Some family and friends simply disappear out of discomfort and uncertainty on how to be present with our pain. Other times, we remove ourselves from once close relationships after repeated painful judgments and criticisms for how we are handling our grief.

With the death of our babies comes layer upon layer of loss and grief and shattered certainties. I can't help but wince a little when I hear people talk about how natural and normal it is for a woman's body to get pregnant and to give birth. This is an easy thing to say and to think when you've only known pregnancy to end in joy and life. When your pregnancy ends in silence and stillness, hearing how natural and normal it is can unleash a powerful wave of guilt and shame.

Twelve and six years after the deaths of my daughters, I still struggle with a deep sense of shame for my body's failure to give birth to a living child. I still wrestle with the anger of having been let down by the so-called natural function of a woman's body. I continue to live with the guilt of having no cause or reason for why my body couldn't carry my children into life. I've often heard people joke that a parent's only real job is to get their kid to adulthood alive. I couldn't even bring my girls into this world to take a single breath.

I used to think that I was the only one who struggled in this way. Over the years of working with other mothers like me and talking with the mothers for this book, I've come to realize this feeling is more common than not. Far too many mothers live with this sense of shame and failure festering deep within. This lingering shame is often fueled by constant assertions of how natural and normal pregnancy and birth are for women.

The counselor part of me, the intellectual part of my brain, knows I am not to blame. I tell myself over and over that I did all I could, that I am a loving mother who would have given my own life to save theirs. It doesn't matter that I would never in any way blame another mother like myself for the loss of their baby. It doesn't matter that my logical brain can rationalize how untrue this sense of failure is. The shame, guilt, and aching sense of failure continue to simmer deep inside.

I'm aware that my issues with this body of mine go back much further than her failure to birth my children. This body and I have a lifetime of conflict in our history. But it's her failing of my children I have never been able to forgive.

There are moments when I stare at the belly that once cradled my babies and imagine ripping it out of me in anger and shame and grief. There are times I want to tear at it, to punish this body for its failure and the shame of feeling less than whole as a woman.

This body of mine was once home to my daughters. The womb that once cradled them, and all the love and joy that they were, now feels dark and heavy with grief, shame, and guilt. As much as I feel this body has failed me and regardless of how angry I feel toward it, I cannot destroy the only earthly home my daughters ever knew. This body that failed them, and me, also holds the only remaining cells of their life – those tiny pieces of them that continue to live in me.

So, every day I struggle to reconcile how my body could have both given me the most precious gifts – my children – and so cruelly taken them away. I know now that I am not the only mother who struggles with this. This knowledge both comforts me to know that I am not alone and deeply saddens me to know so many other women also feel this way.

Jennifer described a similar feeling, *"The biggest hindrance is feeling alone. I started to heal more when I realized there were other women like me. I didn't know anyone else with late term loss or death in delivery. I felt so ashamed until I found others like me."*

What hovers over that hidden storm of shame and guilt are bolts of raging anger and searing jabs of jealousy and envy. One of the things I remember most clearly about the first year after my daughter Grace died, other than the sensation of my world imploding, is a simmering rage that would overwhelm me without warning. The smallest of things could set off this rage inside of me, a feeling so intense it often made me afraid of myself and what I might be capable of doing. Any simple irritant – someone driving too slowly in traffic, forgetting to brush my teeth, an annoying fidgety person next to me in class - had the potential to bring up this fury inside of me about the unfairness of life and *wrongness* of living in a world without my baby.

There were days when the silent screaming inside my head was so loud I couldn't hear those around me. I was always afraid that someday I wouldn't be able to keep it inside and that others would see this raging wildness in me. I used to spend hours sitting in a local coffee shop, frozen in place and staring blindly out the window. Inside, I was desperately trying to contain this overwhelming sense of anger and wrongness, terrified that if I let it out, there would be no end to it.

Over time, as that rage did slowly ease, what came in its place was a paralyzing depression and thoughts of suicide. I couldn't reconcile in my mind how I could still be in this world - breathing, walking, talking, moving, and living – while my baby was dead. I didn't want to exist in a world that my baby did not. Looking back now, I'm not entirely sure whether or not I was actively suicidal. However, I do remember near constant thoughts that I didn't want to be here without her and feeling as if life would be better for everyone if I simply wasn't here anymore either. Most days, it took all the strength I had merely to get out of bed. On the outside, I was functioning well in the world. I was going to class, going to work, engaging with friends and roommates, and living the appearance of a normal life. Inside, I felt hollow and empty, broken and scattered. I was functioning, but not fully present. I felt numb, as if I was a shadow moving through the world, but not fully alive.

For a period of time after each of my daughter's deaths, being around babies and children or pregnant women was almost unbearable. Seeing them brought up that shame of my body's inability to bring my children safely into the world. I would see other mothers and think, "Why you and not me? What did I do wrong?" It was a painful, devastating reminder of what I had lost. The jagged edges of anger and jealousy felt crazy and irrational.

Jealousy is a common occurrence for many invisible mothers. Jealously for having been denied that which we most wanted. The envy of having to watch by the sidelines as so many other mothers carry healthy babies to term with seeming ease and naivety. Even today, years after the loss of my children, I feel envious of the blissful innocence of so many mothers who get pregnant easily and experience uneventful pregnancies, of those mothers who have never really worried about the possibility of their baby dying.

I hear some mothers talk about how great they felt during pregnancy and how powerful they felt during their labor, how natural and beautiful it was to feel their child grow within them. I can't help but feel a wave of grief and jealousy for never having known that kind of pregnancy and birth. Both of my pregnancies were riddled with grief, fear, and intense anxiety. On the flip side, for many of us, hearing mothers complain about the challenges of their pregnancies or children can fill us with rage. It can feel unbearable to listen to another complain about an experience we would give anything to be having with our children.

It's hard, I think, for loved ones to understand how painful it can be to hear of their pregnancies, watch their bellies grow and see their living, breathing, healthy babies when we are haunted by the memories of blood and death, stillness and silence. Baby showers and birthday parties are like minefields littered with pain and grief, jealousy and wrenching loss.

This jealousy so many invisible mothers experience isn't rational. It isn't really fair because the "visible mothers" haven't done anything wrong. You have every right to celebrate and be happy about your pregnancy and children. We know that. Grief, however, isn't logical or rational. Especially in the early years after this loss, the hugeness of these emotions – anger, jealousy, sadness, anxiety – can make even the simplest of life activities feel overwhelming. Add on the bitter pain of being around pregnant mothers and young children and it can simply be too much. We may say no to attending your baby showers, children's birthdays, or refrain from visiting after your baby has been born because of this. Please don't take this personally. Our choice not to attend isn't because we don't love you or want to support you. It's simply that in trying to cope with our own grief we have nothing left to give. We are learning how to navigate this new world without our babies and sometimes the best we can do is get out of bed in the morning.

For many mothers, behind the jealousy and anger, lingers a deep sense of being left out. We are mothers, yet not in the traditional way. We are childless, but not by choice. We are lost in a sort of limbo and we don't quite fit anywhere.

One mother shared, *"I'm tired of feeling different. I don't accept me or my situation as I am. I feel left out of both worlds. I don't have a living child yet I'm not childless by choice either. Where do I belong?"*

Kim put it this way, *"I often feel alienated or invisible, as if because I don't have my child here with me, I am somehow not a "real adult" yet. The sense of not belonging is terribly painful."*

Dear Amelia,

I miss you! It has been 18 months since you quietly slipped into and out of this world and I miss you as much today as I did on January 7, 2014, the day you were born sleeping.

As much as I miss you, I am so thankful that you are my daughter and that you made me a mom. So many people don't understand that but your life, however short, made me a mom and for that I am so thankful. Your life is important and I will celebrate you until the day that I die.

I wish that you could have stayed longer. I wish that I was running around after you and never knowing the pain and emptiness that comes from missing you. Instead, I feel you in the wind and see you in the ocean and trees that surround us. I pick up heart rocks on my beach walks and trust that they are your messages to me until we meet again in some way.

I love you and will always love you, my dear sweat daughter.

Love,

Mom

We are mothers,
yet not in the traditional way.
We are childless, but not by choice.
We are lost in a sort of limbo
and we don't quite fit anywhere.

unseen

What You Don't See

—————

One of the most challenging things about finding and receiving the needed support after this kind of loss is the pervasive silence and invisibility of it. For a myriad of reasons, it took me more than six years to even tell anyone about the life and death of my daughter Grace. It took me several years longer to begin to talk about her and my loss openly. I can't even begin to imagine how my life might have been different had I opened up sooner. Perhaps the years of depression and suicide would not have been, perhaps I might have been happier, more loving, more engaged, and had better relationships.

I used to think my experience was unusual, that it was uncommon to have been pregnant and have no one know and therefore feel as if I couldn't tell anyone about the loss of her. The exact circumstances for me were perhaps a little unusual, but the silence and hidden nature of this loss is not so unusual. There is this saying that I hear too often, especially in medical circles, about how it's "safe to tell after 12 weeks." This idea comes from the belief that miscarriage and pregnancy loss are most common in the first trimester and that it's better to wait until you are "safely" in the second trimester to begin sharing your pregnancy openly.

Well, I call bullshit on that myth.

First, babies can and do die at any point throughout pregnancy. Statistically speaking, more babies die before 12 weeks, yes, but babies do also die after 12 weeks and even during birth. In fact, in 2014 the Center for Disease Control released a report showing that babies in the United States die more frequently than babies in any of the other top 25 wealthy countries in the world. A baby born in the U.S. is less likely to see his first birthday than one born in Cuba or Slovakia. Believing that 12 weeks is the magic number of safety is misleading and can create a false sense of security once that number has passed. Many women I've talked with who experienced the death of their babies after 12 weeks of pregnancy, talked about being angry because no one had even told them that baby loss could happen after 12 weeks. Very few doctors or midwives discuss the risks of miscarriage or stillbirth with mothers at all.

One mother reported, *"I didn't realize stillbirth even happened anymore. Babies don't just die in the womb."*

Second, creating an environment in which pregnancy is hidden until after the "safe" 12 week mark has been reached, contributes significantly to the silence and isolation of losing your baby. What happens when a couple decides to wait until after 12 weeks to share their pregnancy, but their baby dies prior to that? This scenario creates uncertainty and gives rise to difficult questions such as:

No one knew we were pregnant, do we tell them now that our baby has died?

How do we tell our family and friends that our baby was here but is gone now?

Who do we share our pregnancy and loss with?

Would it be easier to just not say anything?

This idea that couples should wait to share their pregnancy until after it's "safe" at 12 weeks can lead to significantly less support and awareness around the loss. The grieving process can be hindered by reduced support from family and friends, as well as employers, who may not even know about the pregnancy, let alone the loss.

The truth is, babies can and do die at any point during pregnancy or birth. The truth is that a parent should share the news of a pregnancy as early or late in the process as *they* desire. Sharing the news of a pregnancy early could mean that news of the baby's death will have to be shared, but it may also mean that parents receive better support through their grief process.

The responsibility for helping to break the silence and isolation around babies who die during pregnancy and the grief of those parents belongs to all of us. It's up to everyone - both the mothers (and fathers) who lose their children and the family and friends who surround them. As mothers without our children, it's up to us to share our experiences, our grief, our love, and our wants and needs. It's up to our loved ones to be there and to listen.

More than anything, those who lose their babies deserve to have the choice to talk or not talk without worrying about sacrificing relationships or support in the process.

As family and friends of loved ones moving through loss, it's important to be present, to listen without judgment, to offer love and support, and to be with us. That is why the first part of this book is about sharing some of our experience to help raise awareness of what we go through as well as what we need. The second part of this book is looking at ways that those around us can better support us through the experience of mothering without our children here.

At some point during the writing of this book, I asked the mothers in several online support groups to share what they have trouble talking about and/or what others don't see about living after the death of their baby. These are some of the most common responses to "What You Don't See Is …"

- How much effort it takes to breathe when my arms physically ache to hold my baby.

- That the only thing the same about me is how I look, I'm not who I used to be.

- That some days getting out of bed is the strongest I can be for the day.

- How much it hurts. How hard it is to just carry on …

- How much I hate the new me. I miss my old self.

- How broken and incomplete I feel even though I am smiling.

- The tears that run down my face with every FB pregnancy announcement.

- How strong I am to face a world that forces me to conceal the world of hurt, pain, sadness - things that are part of me now but make society uncomfortable.

- The leap of joy when I hear you say my baby's name.

- The silent tears inside when my baby is forgotten, unmentioned, or brushed aside as unimportant.

- That I wish I'd die in my sleep or get run over or simply disappear.

- How nervous and anxious I've become.

- How much it hurts that most family members no longer ask me how I'm doing.

- My urge to scream when I see a pregnant woman.

- That I don't care about much anymore, everything feels meaningless without her.

- How having to engage with people and pretending that everything is ok is actually a gazillion times more exhausting than just being real.

- My struggle to wake up every morning and start the day or how worn down I am when I return home.

- That what I often need most is just a hug and a silent presence while I cry.

- How I'm raging every day, angry at the world and I don't understand why.

- How it's hard to be excited about things in my life when I know if I had my babies it would not be happening, and then to hear you tell me you're jealous cuts me to the bone.

- How frustrating it can be to have compassion for my body that I clearly see as having failed to develop my child into a healthy little human.

- That I'm not as strong as you think.

- How painful it is to not fit the mold of what society views as a mother.

- How invisible I feel to the world as a mother.

- How afraid I am that everyone but me will forget my child.

- How hollow I've become and that no matter what or how hard I try I can't be the person I was before.

- The monumental effort it takes just to get through some days.

- The deep sense of shame that my body has failed to give birth to a living child.

- Me quietly slipping away to somewhere quiet so I can catch my breath when an innocent conversation breaks my heart again.

- How much I just want to be SEEN as a mother.

- How much I need to know that my baby's life still matters to you.

- That I look for my children in every child I see.

- How much I imagine who my children might have been and the ache that I will never know.

This list could likely go on and take up half this book. There is so much about this experience of being a mother without a living child that isn't talked about and isn't shared, even with those closest to us. It's difficult to know, as an invisible mother, who will be open to listening to our raw and real experience and who is unable to be present with our pain without judgment. Too many of those we once thought would always be there, have disappeared or been unable to acknowledge our grief. None of us want to walk this journey of motherhood and grief alone. We want to share our children and our experiences with you. We want you beside us.

Dear Elliot,

I wrote my first letter to you on September 8, 2014. It was the morning of our 12 week ultrasound –

Dear baby,

Today we get to see you again. It has been 6 weeks since we last saw you. You've grown so much since then. We can't wait to see you. Mommy and daddy have been waiting for you to come along for quite some time. Now that you are finally growing in my tummy, it's a dream come true. We love you so much already. You also have two sweet dogs waiting to give you lots of kisses and watch over you when you are born. You will love them just as much as they will love you. You've been a good little peanut. Keep up the great work.

Love,

Mommy xoxoxo

I thought it would be special for you to have a few letters to read when you were old enough. I did not realize that would be the first of *many* letters that I would write to you. Nor did I know all but one letter would be written after your silent birth.

There are so many things I want you to know. You're the best thing that has ever happened to daddy and me. We are so proud of you. We would do it all over again if we could. We would go through the pain again if it meant being able to hold you one more time. You grew to be a big, strong, beautiful baby. You tried really hard to come into this world alive. Thank you for trying. I am so sorry my body did not allow that to happen.

You have blessed us in so many ways. Even though you are no longer here on earth, you continue to teach us things about life, death, and love. We did not know the true depths of love before you. We look forward to being with you again, the three of us in heaven. We know you are happy and we can't wait to experience that joy with you.

You may not be in our arms, but we know you are still with us. We feel your presence every day. As I write this letter, I feel the warmth of the sun on my skin. I know that's you watching over me. Thank you, my sweet girl. We love you.

Love,
Mommy xoxoxo

We want to share our children
and our experiences with you.
We want you beside us.

lifetime

A Lifetime of Mothering

My house is a very quiet one. I can't say it's overly neat, but it stays relatively clean and the floors are clear of toys and tumbled shoes. My spare bedroom is an office, free of little girl clothes and clutter. It smells of vanilla and lavender instead of the sweet smell of girlhood. My morning awakening comes from an alarm clock set according to my needs and my schedule is determined by my whims and desires, not dictated by a school calendar. I go where I want, when I want without regard for babysitters, bedtimes, and homework. My home and life is filled with quiet, stillness, and freedom.

On the surface, this home and life of mine looks nothing like that of a typical mother. Yet that is what I am. I am a mother of two beautiful girls. They simply don't live on this earth anymore. You can't see my girls and there is no real evidence of their life here on earth. But I see them every day.

I look for pieces of who they might have been in every child I see. There is always a flash, a split second moment, when I walk into my house and I see a floor littered with toys and little girl shoes and hear the whisper of little girl voices. Then the flash is gone and it is simply my quiet home with its clutter-free floors and stillness and empty spaces.

There are nights when I dream of the life I might have experienced had Grace and Lily lived. In the dream, I am loving them, parenting them, learning from them, hugging them, hearing their voices, feeling their touch, and seeing their faces as they grow and live. We are living a typical day of life and school and activities. In my dreams I get to live ordinary moments of an everyday life with my daughters.

Unfortunately, that's not my life. No matter how beautiful the dream, I wake up and my girls die all over again. I wake up weeping wildly for my daughters and the motherhood I'll never have. I have to live the motherhood I do have, without them physically present here with me. This isn't the motherhood I planned or wanted, but it is motherhood. Not even their deaths could take that away from me.

And so it is for many, many other mothers living without any of their children to hold.

To the world around us, our motherhood is deniable. Since others cannot see tangible, physical proof of our children, they often have difficulty seeing our motherhood as well. Because our babies died before, at, or soon after birth, others don't have memories of them outside of the vague sort of told knowledge. They didn't know our babies as we did. Perhaps that is why it is too often easy for others to forget or to dismiss the life and value of our babies.

In some ways though, our motherhood looks very similar to those with living children. The early years after our babies are born are marked with sleepless nights, exhaustion, and the sound of crying. It's just that our sleepless nights are caused by grief and nightmares and trauma. Our exhaustion is from the weight and heaviness of grief and struggling with making sense of a world where the unthinkable is not only possible, but happened to us. The crying we try to calm and soothe is our own wrecking sobs, wild bursts of weeping, and silent tears. We, too, struggle to adjust to a life turned upside down. However, rather than altering our life to accommodate the normal disruption caused by a new baby, we are trying to adjust to the sudden and violent absence of our beloved baby. We are struggling to make sense of the irreversible changes to who we are and our sense of security in the world. We deal with unsolicited advice on how to grieve and heal just as mothers to living children received unsolicited advice on parenting and childcare practices.

We, too, experienced the discomforts of nausea, swollen ankles, heartburn, and fatigue during our pregnancies. We watched our bodies change with a mix of delight and sense of "what the hell is happening to my body?!" Many of us experienced the joy of that first fluttering sensation and the realization that our baby was real and alive inside of us. Some mothers counted kicks, struggled to see their feet, and walked with the uncomfortable waddle that comes in late pregnancy. Others experienced the contractions and pain of labor as we fought to birth our children into this world.

For those of us fortunate to see our baby's tiny bodies, we too, look for resemblances to our own faces in their eyes and noses and chins. We examine their faces and hands and toes to see pieces of ourselves and our partner in their silent and still bodies, to find the physical traits we might have passed on to them. We soak in the sight of them, working to imprint these images on our minds and hearts so that we might remember the look and feel of this baby we love so much for a lifetime without them. For those of us who were never able to see our baby, we can't help but imagine what their faces may have looked like.

Sadly, we get many of the painful and challenging pieces of early motherhood with few of the joys and delightful moments. For us, there are no smiles, no tiny hands to grip our finger, no baby to hold to our breast to nurture, no sound of coos and giggles, and no wail of a cry. Our babies are forever tiny and still. We don't get to watch them grow and learn. We don't get to see their personalities develop and get to know them as toddlers or children or adults exploring this beautiful world of ours. While other mothers talk of the ache of their children growing up too fast, our babies remain forever as babies. They are forever and always our tiny babies whose only known world was our womb or perhaps a few brief days or weeks in a hospital.

This doesn't mean, however, that we don't know our children. They spent the whole of their brief lives with us. We nurtured them, loved them, talked with them, planned for them, and carried them with us always. In the brief time we had with them, we created a bond and a relationship that death cannot undo. Science now shows that some of the cells of babies live within their mother's body forever. While others get to watch their children live and grow outside their bodies, we have to settle for carrying the remaining pieces of our child's life within our bodies for the rest of our physical lives. The knowledge that they always remain part of us can be both a joy and heartache.

We don't get to mother in the usual sense of bath time and feeding, teaching and learning, potty training and sending them off to school. We don't get to give hugs and kisses, tend skinned knees, enforce rules or consequences and teach boundaries or manners. We don't get to watch them take their first step, give them birthday parties, watch them go on their first date, see them graduate from school, or become grandmothers when they have children of their own. This is not our way of mothering.

Our mothering is less tangible and less visible than that. I don't remember many details of the delivery of my Grace, but I vividly recall being so determined to do it well. Throughout my labor and delivery all I could think was that this was the only thing I would ever be able to do for her, the only way I would mother her in this world. Once her body was born, there would be nothing tangible left for me to do in this lifetime. I could bring her into this world and, as all mothers eventually do for their kids, I also had to let her go. They were equally important acts of mothering and the only "normal" ones I would ever do for her. I just had to do them both at the same time.

How I mother now, of course, looks very different. My motherhood isn't visible. You can't look at my life and see my daughters or how I mother them, although mothering them is what I do every day. My motherhood isn't about hugs or setting boundaries, homework or teaching manners, handling temper tantrums or teenage rebellion. Instead, my motherhood is about living my life in a way that honors their lives. With everything I do, I ask myself, "Is this choice honoring them?" "Am I being someone they would be proud to call their mom?" "Am I living my life to the fullest to celebrate their lives?" Like any mother, I am imperfect and make mistakes, but everything I do is because of them.

In some ways, I have raised a thousand daughters. In my mind I have lived a thousand lifetimes with them and will live thousands more throughout my life on Earth. I have imagined countless times how I would hold them, love them, teach them, and marvel at them. I have wondered in endless ways about who they would be and what our life might have been.

Sometimes when I picture my Grace she has my red hair, her father's brown eyes, and the shape of my mother's face. Other times, she has dark brown hair with my curls, eyes the same shape as mine and my mother's, and her father's smile. Or a million other combinations of how she might have looked. I picture her with my stubborn determination, her father's sense of humor, a love of books and reading, a passion for music, and a love of animals. The next day I imagine her as a ball of energy, with a love of soccer and dance, a social butterfly always ready to try new things and create new adventures. It's the same with her sister Lily. Would she have red hair or brown? Blue eyes or honey brown? What would her favorite color be? Would she be feisty or sweet or both? Would she talkative or quiet? Every time I see other girls who would be about their age, I can't help but wonder, would my girls be like them? Would they have been friends?

If I close my eyes I can almost hear their laughs, smell their little girl hair, and feel their arms wrap around me as I hug them. I see myself caring for them, making them breakfast, helping them with their homework, comforting them through life's hurts, celebrating their successes, and marveling in the wonder of who they are. I mark every normal life event that they would have experienced in my mind – learning to walk and talk, preschool, making their first friends, learning to read, Halloween costumes they might have worn, holiday traditions we might have created, and everything in between. In my imagination, I am an ordinary mother living an ordinary yet beautiful life with my daughters.

Instead, what I have is a whisper of a possibility that is already gone. I carry endless images and imaginings of who they might be. Every day I ache for knowing that the daughters I imagine in my mind have never and will never exist as I imagine them, not in this world here with me.

I am the mother of two very real babies who changed my life forever and a thousand invisible children who might have been. For all of us who feel like invisible mothers, our beautiful babies who leave too soon make us mothers. We are mothers forever to the babies they were and the children they might have become.

A mother's love never dies.

We are mothers forever
to the babies they were
and the children
they might have become.

Part Two:

Sharing Love and Support

Sharing Love and Support

I picked up my first book about grief and loss when I was fifteen years old. It's probably safe to say that trying to understand grief and how to heal from it has been a lifelong journey. I often feel that I came into this life for that purpose. What I have learned from my own experiences with loss and from my lifetime of professional study is that everyone grieves in their own unique way. No one can say with absolute confidence that "this is what you will experience" or "this is the process you will go through."

There are no stages, no orderly steps, and no timeline to predict anyone's grief process. It affects each of us differently. My philosophy of grief is that we must all carve our individual path through life with grief.

Similarly, we react to different losses in different ways. We may grieve one way following the death of our first child and differently after the loss of our second. Simply put, grief is unpredictable.

Keeping that in mind may provide the opportunity to open up a conversation with someone you love. This could be your chance to understand their unique process more fully by talking with them what they are experiencing – not just once, but often as they move and evolve through this process called living while grieving.

understanding

A Foundation of Understanding

The foundation of my work around grief and loss for mothers who live without any of their children is simple:

- Our babies' lives have meaning and value.

- Our lives and experience of motherhood is valuable and meaningful.

Caitlin put it beautifully, *"At first I looked for purpose and meaning in his life. Then I realized that the fact that he lived was enough."*

That's it. That's the fundamental building block of everything any of us need to know about supporting those in our lives (including ourselves) who have experienced this painful loss. Our babies lived and that's value enough.

When I first started my grief counseling practice and began to share my experience of losing my daughters, every single time I spoke about them publicly, countless other women would approach me and share their stories. Many of the mothers who had lost their babies decades before would tell me that they had never before talked about the loss of their baby. They had been told early on, it was "just a miscarriage" or "just a fetus" or "just a stillbirth" and to simply "get over it and forget."

These mothers would share their stories and cry for the relief of being heard and seen for the first time. Being told their babies did matter and did have value helped release years of silent grief and hidden sorrow.

We know it isn't easy to be with us with our pain and grief. It isn't easy for anyone to see loved ones hurting and in such incredible pain. We get that it's not a fun or easy topic to discuss. Too often we are so intensely aware of how uncomfortable it is for you that we present ourselves as ok and struggle to hide our pain from you. We might pretend it's ok to not talk about it because we don't want you to feel badly.

At the same time, you may be not bringing up our loss or our children because you don't want to cause us any more pain when we seem to be "doing better." You may avoid the topic of our children or not reach out on anniversaries or birthdays because you want to protect us from more grief or pain. Trust us: we are already feeling grief and pain, and if anything, *not* reaching out makes it worse.

Debra shared, *"Even though I'm not crying or saying it out loud anymore, doesn't mean I don't think about it. It doesn't mean it doesn't still hurt or that I'm over it. It's been 24 years and it's always with me. I don't want her to be forgotten."*

This double-sided attempt to protect each other from pain? It flat out doesn't work. It prevents all of us from reaching out when we need it most. It causes both sides to feel disconnected. It perpetuates isolation and feelings of shame and invalidation. It prevents you from the chance to get to know the new person we've become and are still becoming. Suddenly, neither side is engaged in one another's life and relationships start to falter.

The death of a baby is personal, intimate, and massive on so many levels. No one really wants to think about the death of babies. This kind of loss challenges our beliefs about life, our sense of safety, and our own morality. When we, or someone we love, have a baby who dies all of a sudden the unthinkable is made very real and personal.

The truth is no one really handles this kind of loss well. Even I, despite my experience with my daughters and years of experience as a grief counselor, struggle at times to know what to say or how to be with someone in this level of profound grief. It's uncomfortable, sad, and full of vulnerability.

Discomfort, sadness, and vulnerability are not generally feelings most of us jump into with ease and joy. At best, we brace ourselves with a reluctant acceptance of them. At worst, we run like hell from them, trampling anyone who gets in our way. And because few of us really know how to handle this topic with ease or comfort, hurt runs amuck. Misunderstandings and mistaken assumptions run rampant. People on both sides feel hurt, abandoned, rejected, and judged.

If you are a family member or friend of an invisible mother and you get nothing else from this book, please understand this:

You cannot fix this for us.

Nothing you say or do will take away our grief or our pain over the loss of our child. Grief isn't something that can be fixed, it has to be felt and experienced and moved through.

You can't make everything better for us, but that doesn't mean we don't need your love and support.

We need you to see us.

We need you to acknowledge our motherhood and our babies' lives.

We need you to remember with us.

We need you to be present with us, at our worst and at our best.

We need you to love us, without judgment.

My dearest Erryn Shiloh,

My strong gift. My Angel baby. You are a blessing that entered my life so quickly only to be taken away just as fast. 16 weeks and 6 days was not near long enough when it should have been a life time. I cherish the little memories I do have of you; hearing your heart beat, watching grow and move with the ultrasound, starting to feel you kick.

I wish I could have done more for you; been strong like you and kept holding on. I'm sorry my body failed you, that I couldn't protect you. Your life stolen from you before it even had a chance to start. For that I will never be able to forgive myself. I wish I could hold you in my arms, kiss your cheeks, and whisper I love you until you fall asleep. I regret that the day you were born I never held you. I couldn't bear the thought of holding you and knowing I would have to let you go. It was selfish; I was trying to protect my own heart that was already breaking into a thousand pieces. I pray that you are watching me from above and can forgive me for not being there for you when you needed me the most.

I hope you have found peace and know that you are loved beyond measure. There is not a day that goes by where you are not on my mind. In everything I do I try to honor you and your memory. You are my strong gift, my angel baby, my first born little boy. You are the blessing I prayed for all my life and I am so proud to be your momma. No matter how much time goes by I'll never stop loving you. Never.

I love you, Erryn. Thank you for choosing me to be your momma.

Our babies lived and

that's value enough

platitudes

Ban the Platitudes, Please

I like to believe that most people have good intentions when hurtful statements come out of their mouths after the loss of a child – or any loved one. Generally, I try to assume that they are trying to help and simply are at a complete loss for how to help. I prefer to believe that the hurtful things that often come out of their mouth are the result of anxiety and uncertainty rather than malice or judgment. Good intentions, however, don't take away the pain of hurtful statements or judgments.

So, how can loved ones help without getting sidetracked by their own anxiety, uncertainty, and good intentions? First, be aware of what isn't helpful.

Some of the most common painful statements heard after the death of a baby are things like:

"You're young yet. You'll have another baby."

"At least it was an early miscarriage."

"It was just a miscarriage."

"At least you know you can get pregnant now."

"So and so had X number of miscarriages and now they have X number of children. You just have to keep trying."

Or the religious platitudes including:

"God needed another angel."

"God knows the right time for you to be a mother, just have faith."

"Your baby is an angel now, he/she was just too beautiful for earth."

"We don't always know God's reasoning, but he always has one."

"Your baby is in a better place now."

Folks, no. For the love of kindness, no.

Please kindly remove the words "at least" and "just" from your vocabulary. These statements are invalidating and dismissive of the grief we are experiencing for THIS baby that we lost. Even if we manage to go on and have other living children, those living children cannot replace the baby that we lost. We love *this* baby. We had hopes and dreams for *this* baby. This baby was our child and he/she has died. Please don't devalue their life with "at least" and "just."

It's also important to remember that not everyone shares the same religious or spiritual beliefs. Even if the mother who is grieving her child is a religious person, it's generally better to avoid religious platitudes. The death of a child can create questioning and doubt in even the most faithful of people. It's also important to remember that, religious or not, every mother deserves to grieve for the loss of her baby – whatever her belief about God, angels, and the afterlife. Please don't try to push away someone's grief with reassurances of faith.

Then there is the other big, pink elephant in the room that no one likes to talk about when babies die: *Sometimes, we don't get another baby.*

Even in the baby loss community "rainbow babies" often dominate the discussion. Rainbow babies are babies born after the "storm" or the death of a baby. There is too often an assumption, spoken or unspoken, that everyone will go on to have their rainbow baby and all will be well. We are told to "have faith," because someday, of course, we all get to be mothers to a living child.

This is a painful and inaccurate myth. These rainbow babies get talked about as if they are a certainty – something many of us as invisible mothers know all too well isn't the case. Many families struggle with infertility or secondary infertility. Their initial pregnancy may have been a seeming miracle after years of trying to conceive. Then their miracle baby died. They are all too well aware that they may or may not ever get pregnant again.

Others do get pregnant with their rainbow baby, and then that baby dies as well. This is exactly what happened with my Lily, who died after her older sister, Grace. Many mothers I talked with had loss after loss after loss, trying again and again to become a mother to a living child only to have to say good-bye to every baby who came. Then they find themselves entering menopause or needing to have a hysterectomy and facing the heartbreaking realization that they will never have living children. Other mothers have multiple losses and find they cannot bear to face the possibility of losing another baby and choose to stop trying.

There is often an underlying belief that healing from the death of a baby requires having another baby or having a living child born before loss. This is a false belief. There can be healing without a living child. When other loss mothers say things such as "I couldn't have survived if I hadn't had my older child" or "I don't know what I would have done if I hadn't finally had my rainbow baby" it is devastating and invokes a sense of hopelessness in mothering without living children. These kinds of statements only hurt invisible mothers more. As Raeanne put it, *"If this is true, where is my hope and healing if I can't have another baby?"*

And let me say again - even if mothers do go on to have living children, it does not mean that they suddenly are healed and don't grieve for the baby who died. A new baby cannot replace the baby who died. We don't grieve simply for "a baby," we grieve for *our baby*, that specific baby who came and then left. Another baby would be loved and cherished, but will not take the place of our baby who died. When someone experiences the death of their teenage child, no one says to them, "Well, you can just have another child and everything will be fine." No, we know that no one can replace that teenager. It is no different for those of us who lose our children during pregnancy or infancy. Yet this is the message that mothers who have babies die during pregnancy often receive.

Please, please, refrain from trying to reassure us that we will have another baby. You can't know that. And we are now all too familiar with the unpredictability of life – the death of our beloved babies taught us that with sudden and clear certainty. Don't try to push us past this current loss by projecting into a future neither of us can predict.

Then we have the popular adoption fix. *"Just adopt! There are lots of babies waiting for families."* Or *"You would be such a great mother. Why don't you just adopt instead?"*

Adoption is a wonderful option and has brought many beautiful families together. However, to blithely tell a mother or couple struggling to have a child, "Well, you can just adopt!" (Note the dismissive use of "just" again here) is generally unhelpful and simplistic. Adoption is a complicated and expensive process. As much as many families might love to adopt a child as their own, not everyone has the resources available or legal ability to do so.

A woman once blithely gushed about how great of a mother I would be and how it would be "such a pity" if I weren't to have any children. She was insistent that if I "didn't want" to have children of my own I needed to adopt. At the time I was wrestling emotionally with the choice to let go of the idea of having living children, by birth or adoption. I had finally given myself permission not to take the emotional risk having to say good-bye to another child and had made the choice to not have any more children. Her words only created more pain and self-doubt. They did nothing to support or comfort me.

We know it isn't easy to figure out how to support us through this painful grief process. We understand you might not know what to say or do.

Honestly, neither do we. No words can fix this loss. It's ok to recognize and acknowledge that without trying to gloss over it.

My Dearest Sofie:

I loved you since the moment I knew you were inside me, my beautiful princess. I have never experienced such joy and love for anyone up to this point and have not experienced it since. All the times you, my princess, would move inside me, and the kicks you did, oh how I cherished them. I had so many plans and hopes for the life we would have together. I so wish it hadn't been cut so short. There are some days still, that I so wish and hope we could have more time together. And I will always wonder who you would have become. But I know I need to cherish the short time we had together. And I do, Sofie, I do cherish that time we had together.

We were the only ones who felt each other's heart beat's. There is a bond that will never go away and will stay forever.

I miss you so much my sweet princess. Mommy lives everyday for the both of us, Sofie Olivia.

Until the day we meet again Sofie, mommy misses you so much and you are in my heart always.

Love,

Your Mommy Audrey

No words can fix this loss.
It's ok to recognize and
acknowledge that.

*presence &
honesty*

Bring Your Presence and Your Honesty

In my experience, simpler is best. Supporting us through this heart shattering loss isn't as complicated as we tend to think it is.

Be with us.

Bottom line, that's all it really takes. Sit with us. Hug us while we cry. Listen to us talk about our babies or our experience - open-heartedly and without judgment. Remember our babies' birthdays as you do other family members. Say their names out loud.

Be present with us. Not just for those first few months or that first year. You may feel that we should be moving on more quickly than we are. You may feel that after a few months or a year, we should be more "normal" again. We want you to believe us when we say that's not possible. We will never again be the person you knew. The person that you used to know died when our baby died. This process of learning to live without our children is a *lifelong* process. Our babies are our babies forever. We miss them for as long as we love them – for always.

Rose stated, *"It's been 30 years since my babies died and it still hurts. I wish it had been acknowledged and that people understood it's for a lifetime."*

Perhaps one of the most important things for you to know is that you don't have to understand our loss in order to love and support us. Unless you are an invisible mother, you can't understand our loss. Even among those of us who are invisible mothers, there are vast differences. While it may be challenging to understand why after such lengths of time and so many years we might still miss and grieve for our babies so deeply, remember that your understanding isn't necessary. Your presence and love is. Love us and show us that love, even when you don't understand our grief.

Heather said it simply, *"You don't necessarily have to understand my loss – be compassionate and understand that I am in pain."*

Ryann had this to add, *"Please don't say things like 'I understand what you're going through' or 'I know what you're feeling.' Trying to relate when you can't isn't helpful. Listening and comforting is better than trying to relate or talk."*

If tears come up after five years, hug us and tell us you love us. When we need to talk about them 10 years from now, listen and remember with us. When our baby would be turning 16, remember their birthday with us and acknowledge who they might have been.

Trying to rush us through this process of learning to live with loss or trying to reassure us that the future will be better is achingly unhelpful. As backwards as it sounds, being honest about the uncertainty and depth of this experience is much more soothing than false assurances.

Admit to us that you don't know if we'll ever have another living baby and that it hurts to live with that uncertainty. Acknowledge that this loss is excruciating and give us permission to take all the time we need to heal. Acknowledge the fact that our life has forever changed and cannot be the same as it once was. Recognize with us that the person we used to be will never be again, not in the same way.

Sugarcoating the magnitude and intensity of losing a child helps no one. Attempting to gloss over our experience only serves to create more shame, more guilt, and more disconnection. We know that you can't fully understand this experience, but please don't try to sugarcoat it with vague promises of how much better things will be someday in the future. The future will come and it may very well be beautiful and brilliant, but in those early years after loss, that future sunshine seems too far out of reach to bring any kind of comfort. Optimism in those early months and years can feel blindingly painful.

Instead, if you don't know what to say to us, tell us that. If you don't know what to do for us, say that. If you are at a loss for words, admit that. No one is supposed to know how to handle this, because babies aren't supposed to die. But babies do die and this experience leaves all of us grasping for how we're supposed to navigate and survive.

It's ok if you don't know what to say or do after our baby dies. Neither do we. As Sandy put it, *"Just be there to listen. You don't have to talk, let us talk instead."*

If you can't be present with us, if you can't stand with us in our grief, please be honest about that, too. Maybe you are struggling with your own losses and can't bear to be witness to more. Maybe you simply don't have the emotional strength or capacity at this time, for whatever reason, to give to us. It's ok to say, "I can't be your person for this." It's ok to say to us, "I love you and I want to support you, but I can't be what you need right now." It may be hard for us to hear, but kind honesty is infinitely better than not knowing why you suddenly and inexplicably disappeared from our life or feeling pressured to be better, faster, to soothe your discomfort.

All we want is for you to love us. Demonstrate that love with your presence and your kind honesty.

Dear Olivia,

You should be 2 1/2 right now, getting into things and learning to say No. You should still be nursing now and then. You should be dropping mispronounced F-bombs when you see a truck.

But you're here only in Daddy's heart and my heart, and the hearts of those who love us.

I wish you were here. Every day I miss you, and I look around my life and think, this isn't how it was supposed to be.

We were supposed to have to build a third stall on the barn for the pony you'd ride in the leadline class at Devon next summer. We were supposed to have a swingset in the yard. I was supposed to still need that car seat. You were supposed to be keeping us a awake at odd hours.

I miss you. I wish you were here. I have found new ways to fill the empty hours, I have found new friends and new purposes, new reasons to get up in the morning, and I love those things.

But I would trade them all in an instant, for you to be here with me.

Love,
Mama

All we want is for you to love us.

remember

Remember With Us

O ne of the things I heard over and over again in my interviews for this book was how much mothers love to hear people say their baby's name. There is no sweeter sound than hear their name spoken out loud, to have our beautiful babies recognized and remembered in the world.

Paula talked about how only a couple friends ever say her daughter Olivia's name. She shared that one of the greatest gifts a friend has given her is his willingness to say Olivia's name and talk about Olivia with her.

Many family members and friends of those who are grieving have told me that they often hesitate to talk about the baby who died or aren't sure if they should mention anything about the loss or baby. Usually, this uncertainty is about not wanting to upset their loved one or to cause them any additional hurt or pain.

The truth is, it's the silence around our babies that causes the additional hurt and pain. The very spark that sent me on the path to writing this book was the fear and grief that no one else would remember my daughter, that her life would be forgotten and lost to the world. That was a pain I couldn't bear to know.

Ann stated, *"Even though I'm not crying or talking about her as much, doesn't mean I don't think about her. It doesn't mean I don't hurt anymore. I want to talk about her, but I feel like no one wants to listen."*

Don't be afraid to ask about our babies or how we are doing. Don't be afraid to remember them and to share the things that make you think of them. We may cry or tear up, yes, but not because you are hurting us – rather, we are so grateful that you remember. We hurt already. We are already thinking about them. Speaking their name to us and remembering our babies with us is a gift. Gift us often with the sweet sound of their name.

When you remember with us on birthdays and holidays, when you acknowledge their life on those special days and on other ordinary days, you give us a priceless gift. To know our sweet, deeply loved babies are remembered, valued, and honored brings a comfort words cannot describe.

One mother stated, *"When you acknowledge these days, it means more than anything in the world. It means that she was alive to someone other than me."*

It brings me great joy when friends or loved ones say to me, "I'm remembering Grace with you today" on her birthday or "thinking of you and Lily this month" in June, the month that I call "Lily's Month."

I think perhaps the biggest fear of an invisible mother is that our children will be forgotten. It was an unbearable thought for me, the day I realized I'd never heard anyone speak my Grace's name and if I were to die, no one would remember her at all. Her existence would simply vanish from the world's memory and no one would know the value of her too-brief life. Hearing her name spoken aloud by others soothes that fear inside my heart and brings great comfort.

Help us make sure our children are not forgotten. Remember their birthdays. Acknowledge them at holiday gatherings. Include them in your count of grandchildren and nieces/nephews. Tell us when you see or hear something that makes you think of them.

The value of you remembering our babies and acknowledging them cannot be overstated. You can give us no greater comfort than to let us know our babies matter to you, too.

Dear Finley,

When I was pregnant with you, I was truly in a blissful state of happiness. Sure, the morning sickness was hard and being in a new country was difficult, but from the moment your daddy and I found out that you were going to be joining our family, we began truly living for you.

We had so many hopes and so many dreams that only continued to grow as time went on. Each perfect ultrasound and each happy movement that you made only solidified the future that we were building in our minds and in our home. There is no way that we ever could have predicted that you wouldn't be coming home with us after you were born.

We had everything ready for you; so much time was spent choosing every little item that would be yours or would be used in your care. So much love went into those decisions. We wanted you to have the best that we were able to give.

The night you were born was the most important and life changing moment of my life. You made me a mother, Finley. Truly there is no bigger change that a woman can go through, and it hurts so much that I never got to see our relationship grow as you grew. I think I would have been a good mother if you had lived, as I try to be a good mother to you even now.

I was never scared about the fact that we'd have a baby to care for. I don't think your daddy was either. We were excited. I've never seen your daddy so excited, or seen his eyes light up the way they did when we were making plans for the future. It breaks my heart that you aren't here to learn from him. He is wonderful with children, and I know he would be even better with you.

Even now, over three years after you died, I have a parallel life in which I imagine where we would be if you had lived. I imagine what you'd look like, what you would sound like, what it would feel like to get a sloppy kiss from you and feel your little arms around my neck. I imagine hearing you say "I love you mummy" and it fills my heart more than could ever know.

I love you, Finley, and I miss you so much.

Sleep tight little man.

Love,
Mummy xx

You can give us no greater comfort

than to let us know

our babies matter to you, too.

see

See Our Motherhood

One of the most challenging things about being an invisible mother is, well, the invisibility of it. To the world around us, we don't appear to be mothers. There is no physical evidence of our children – no diapers and toys, no messy cars or overstuffed backpacks, no living, breathing, active child that you can see as evidence of our motherhood.

For us, there is no simple or pain-free answer to the question, "Do you have children?" The internal debate to this question can be intense.

Do I say yes and explain?
Do I just say yes, but then what if they ask how old he/she is?

Do I have the energy to go through the story all over again?

Maybe I should just say no, but I always feel so guilty when I do that.

What is her/his reaction going to be if I say I have a child but he/she is dead?

I want to acknowledge my child but I don't want to deal with their discomfort and that awkward silence.

Gah, I hate this question.

Too often our children's lives have been dismissed or invalidated because they cannot be seen or were not experienced by anyone other than us. Knowing who we can trust to share their lives, and our motherhood, with can be challenging. One mother talked about how cautious she is about sharing her daughter with just anyone – just as she would be cautious about handing her daughter off to just anyone if her daughter was still living.

As a professional, I started replacing the question, "Do you have children?" with "Do you have any living or deceased children?" Some people, who have not lost a child, find my version of this question startling. However, I can often see a visible relief on the faces of those who have, because they know instantly that I "count" and validate the life of their deceased child.

In the same light, our experience of pregnancy or birth is often dismissed or disregarded. People rarely want to hear us share our experience of pregnancy or birth when they know that it ended in silence and death. Often, others who are uncomfortable or afraid to acknowledge the reality that babies can die shut down those invisible mothers who desire to share their stories of pregnancy or birth.

Mother's Day comes with weeks of being bombarded by ads, commercials, and pictures of carefree mothers holding their children. Nowhere among them is our motherhood represented or acknowledged. Rarely do we receive cards or recognition on this painful day. Churches and spiritual centers gush about and praise mothers for the challenges of raising children, but rarely take a moment to honor the challenges of mothering children that cannot be seen or held or touched.

Careless remarks of "you need to get working on having those babies before it's too late" or "you'll make the best mother someday" or "I bet your parents can't wait for those grandbabies" leave us feeling wounded, scarred, and unbelievably invisible. Too often we are already trying to have children or have lost our babies and you simply aren't aware of it.

I would encourage us all to remember, as we walk through our lives, that not everything about us can be seen. Not all of who we are is apparent in the visible world. You may not be able to see our children, but we are mothers.

One of the most healing moments in my journey of grief after the death of my daughter Grace came when I finally broke my silence on her death and talked about her with a dear teacher and friend. This woman was the first person to acknowledge me as a mother. That simple act was like lighting a candle in the dark. It broke through years of sorrow and brought a sense of lightness and freedom to my spirit.

In a similar way, it has brought me great joy and comfort in recent years to receive messages from my mother wishing me Happy Mother's Day. It is a message that brightens an often painful and lonely day.

See us.

Acknowledge our motherhood.

Recognize how deeply we love our children.

Some mothers have their children by their side.

We have ours in our hearts.

But truly we are not so different from each other.

We are all mothers.

Dear Hannah Sue,

I love you. I want nothing more than to hold you close. I miss you with all my heart and soul.

I often imagine what your life would be like and what mine would be like if I had you here. There is so much I wish I knew. So much I want to experience with you. I want to watch you grow up and experience life.

What type of personality would you have? I imagine stubborn like your Daddy and me. Also gentle, kind, and shy like me; strong and artistic like your Daddy. I'm pretty sure you would be huge lover of animals, babies, and all that sparkles of course. I know you would have been a sweet, caring, and loving little girl and eventually woman.

What you would look like now and as you grew? I know you had my lips and your Daddy's and my hair color. I'm not sure where you got your adorable little nose; Maybe from a grandmother? I try so hard to see you as you would be today. I see you with beautiful long hair and porcelain skin. What color are your eyes? I image blue or even green. Maybe I would have been surprised to find out your eyes were brown or hazel.

What fun and precious memories would I have made with you? I find myself enjoying special moments with family and friends wishing you were there. Outings with friends I often find myself thinking how you should be with me and wondering how you would have behaved. Those precious times with my own Mom, your Nana, I pretend in my mind what it would be like to have you there with us. I long to have those cherished mother and daughter moments with you, Hannah.

Oh Hannah, I love you so much and I always will. You are perfect to me. You are my baby girl. I know our journey isn't a storybook fairy; but it's our journey and I wouldn't trade it for the world if it meant not having you at all. You made me a Mother.

Love Always,
Mommy

I would encourage us all to remember,
as we walk through our lives,
that not everything about us
can be seen.

honoring

Honoring Our Differences

I used the royal "we" frequently in this book, particularly this second section. I am aware that there are vast differences in what each of us need, want, and experience through this process of living without our children. For each and every thing I have written, there can be and likely are, exceptions. Not every invisible mother will agree with the statements and experiences detailed in this book.

And that's okay. This book isn't the end-all-be-all rulebook for supporting grieving mothers. It's a guide to provide points of awareness as you navigate this experience with us.

Again, it is important to acknowledge that there is no set way to grieve. We all grieve differently. We all experience this loss through our own worldviews and life experiences and belief systems. Our experiences are as different as they might be similar.

For those supporting us, this important to remember. Each of us handles loss and death and grief in our own unique way – and even as well as we might know someone, it's difficult to predict how this kind of loss will be experienced.

Remember to listen.

Sometimes, we don't always know how to describe what it is we are feeling. We might not have the right words to ask for what it is we need. Your patience and your willingness to listen openly as we fumble to express ourselves is essential. I remember one year when I tried to talk with a friend about how I was struggling with Mother's Day. Asking for support has never been easy for me and I freely admit I was having trouble articulating what I wanted to say. I certainly wasn't doing a great job asking for the support I needed. Her response was something like "I thought you were past this. I thought things were better now."

Looking back now, I can see that she was likely doing her best to understand and trying to be supportive. At the time, I felt as if I was being judged and criticized for the fact that I was still having a hard time with Mother's Day. I immediately shut down and was unable to talk any further. Having been told so often that I needed to move on and to get over my grief I was extra sensitive to any perceived disregard for my feelings.

What might have helped both of us stay open and continued the conversation so that we both felt supported and understood is to simply say, "Can you tell me more about that?"

The best way to learn how to support the people we love is to listen to them. Let them share what they are experiencing and take cues from what we learn from their sharing. When they say they are hurting, believe them and offer love. When they say they doubt their faith or the world or the science they have always leaned on, listen without judgment. When they rage against the unfairness of it all, stand firm as their anchor in the storm. When they cry for the longing and ache of missing their baby, give them a shoulder to lean on.

My process of grief may look nothing like yours. Yours may look nothing like mine. We are all different and all paths of grief and love are perfect in their expression. But we all want to feel loved.

If you don't know how to help, ask. "How can I support you right now?" is a great question. If they don't have an answer, take a deep breath. Offer a concrete suggestion such as:

"I would love to bring you dinner next week. Would that be helpful to you?"

"How about I take care of your yard this week so you don't have to worry about it. Would that be helpful?"

"I was thinking of giving to the March of Dimes in your baby's honor. Would that be helpful or is there another organization you would

prefer that I support?"

"I'm heading to the grocery store and I would like to pick up some things for you. What can I get for you?"

One mother shared, *"The best thing a friend did was ask, 'Do you want to talk about her? How would you like me to refer to her?' I loved that she asked and didn't just assume I didn't want to talk about her."*

Offer. Ask. Be present.

Listen.

It's enough.

My Fiery Lily,

My feisty girl. You were quite the surprise for Mama! I will admit, I was so afraid to love you. When you were with me, I used to sit outside in the dark and watch the fireflies. Those tiny, light-filled beings reminded me of light and hope and possibility.

You brought all that back to my life. You were my second chance and I couldn't help but fall in love with you. You woke me up. You shook loose all the sorrow I was clinging to so tightly and brought firelight to the darkness.

Our time together was so very brief. It felt as if all the light in the world left with you. But like your sister, you became my teacher. Although I never got to hold you in this life, I carry you with me always. I see you now every June when it seems that you live as the fireflies that light up the dark.

Thank you, my tiny firefly, for bringing back the light. Mama loves you, always.

xoxo,

Mama

We all just want to feel loved.

mother to mother

From Mother to Mother

During the interviews for this book, I asked each mother what advice or encouragement they would give to newly bereaved invisible mothers. Here is some of what they shared:

Amy: "Grief softens. Be proud of your baby and share your story. It's okay to talk about your baby regardless of other people's reactions."

Lisa: "There are things you experience when you lose a baby that make you feel crazy. You aren't crazy, it's just part of the grief process."

Amy: "Your child's life still counts and has an impact on the world. Others might not understand, but it will change you. You are still a carrier and giver of life. Cherish that."

Paula: "Talk about it if you want to. If others can't deal with it, fuck 'em. We, others like you, are out there and you just have to find us."

Rachel: "What you are feeling is okay. You are allowed to feel it. You are not crazy."

Maria: "Go to a therapist or counselor. There are few places that allow us to talk openly about this loss and our child, having a place to do that is very validating. Support groups can be very helpful and help with feelings of being alone."

Lynn: "Please don't feel you can't talk about it. Tell your story. Initially, I felt embarrassed and "less of a woman." But talking and sharing have helped and I've met the most honest and open women sharing their stories too."

Sandy: "Don't feel guilty. It's not your fault."

Veronica: "Listen to yourself – not what the rest of the world wants from you. Do what's best for you."

Kim: "Don't ignore your grief or it will stay bitter instead of eventually fading to bittersweet. Take care of yourself, even if family or friends can't always carry this with us."

Ryann: "You didn't do anything wrong. You were chosen to be this mother and there is just no understanding of why. The greatest thing you can do is hope. Take care of yourself and take care of your partner. Don't worry so much about what others think."

Claire: "Don't let anyone tell you how to grieve. There's no wrong or right way. Let yourself feel what you feel, you can't ignore your feelings."

Debra: "Life does go on, you will smile again and that's okay. Don't feel guilty about feeling okay again. Treasure what memories you have. Don't be afraid to talk about your child."

Michele: "How you are feeling won't last forever. It won't go away, but it will feel easier and you will learn to live without them. Talk as *you* need to. Take it day-by-day. You will laugh and smile again, and that's okay."

Meghan: "It gets different, better in a way. You'll be able to function at some point. Take all the time you need if you can. Seek out support, even if it feels weird. You just have to feel it, there's no way to avoid it."

Chrissy: "People will say a lot of hurtful things. Sometimes it's better to focus on their good intentions and ignore the rest. Give yourself time to grieve. Seek help. Don't be afraid to share your feelings."

Nastashia: "Give it time. Slow down. Feel everything and don't push it away. Don't worry about feeling/being crazy – it's a lot to try to take in."

Kaytlin: "Use the pain as fuel to move forward in your life. Seek out a group or others and tell your story."

Sara: "You are not crazy. These responses are normal. You are trying to make sense and adjust. You are a mother."

Marie: "It can be really, really hard to do, but you can put yourself first. It's okay to be selfish sometimes and this is one of them. Take it at your own pace, it's okay to fall apart. Life will never be the same, but it does go on."

There is no right or wrong way to grieve. Trust your instincts, even when they seem illogical or "crazy." No one can do this but you and so no one's opinion of how it should be done matters except yours.

Trust yourself through this process.

There is no right or wrong way

to grieve.

Life Continues:

A Brighter
Today

As of this writing, my daughters would be twelve and five years old. The loss of them and my identity as their mother has been integrated into my life as a whole – it isn't something I consciously think about most of the time. It simply is who I am. Except on rare occasions, the pain of my grief isn't as cutting or sharp as it was once. Seeing babies or pregnant women doesn't open up a crater of pain inside. Filling out medical forms and responding to the question of whether I have children isn't quite so devastating. I can usually talk about my losses without worrying about whether it makes other people uncomfortable. There remains, however, an ever present sense of something missing and an emptiness that I carry. It's like a vague ache just out of conscious awareness most of the time. Will that ache and emptiness ever completely go away? I don't know. Do I want it to? I don't know that either.

The western culture's attachment to the idea that we should "get over" our grief and loss and that eventually it will "resolve" itself is not one I agree with, as you may have been able to tell through this book. I'm not sure we are meant to get over or resolve the loss of the ones we love. The people we love are integral parts of our lives, of who we are, and who we will yet become. The space that they leave behind, that emptiness we feel when they die is simply an echo of the beauty and love and joy that they brought to our lives. Through their life and their loss, my daughters made my life richer, more beautiful, and more full. They gave life a depth I could never have imagined. I'm not sure I want to "get over" any aspect of that experience.

I stir up a lot of reactions from people with my answer to the question, "If you could go back and change what happened, would you?" Honestly, I don't think I would. I love my daughters and I will always love them. I grieve for them and I still miss their presence and the life we might have had together. I also love who I am now. I love my life now. I love the person they made me through both their lives and their deaths. I love the work I am able to do because of my experience of loving and losing them. I am doing amazing work in the world that I wouldn't have been able to do if they were here. Some have said that I am a selfish or bad mother for feeling this way, but it's my truth and I believe we all deserve to live our truths. I also believe they would have wanted me to live and love my life with or without them. This is part of the both/and living that I believe gives us the capacity to survive and thrive through any circumstance. I can love them, ache for them, and accept their absence all at once.

I would have done anything I could to keep my children here and had they stayed, I would have committed myself to being the best mother I could be to them. In their death and their loss, I have committed myself to being the best mother and person I can be with what I have learned from them. To me, that means living without regrets. I don't regret their brief lives nor do I allow myself to regret their too-soon deaths. The truth is that they aren't physically present in my life. Nothing I do can change that, but I can choose to be happy and to love this life anyway. It might have been easy to stay in the anger and bitterness and darkness of grief after they died. For too many years, I did just that. Then I had to ask myself, is living this way honoring them? I am a mother. I miss my girls more than I could ever express. And I now choose not to have any other children.

Putting the pieces of one's life back together after the devastating death of a baby or child is quite possibly one of the hardest things anyone has to do. It doesn't happen overnight. It doesn't happen in a month. It doesn't happen in a year. It happens over time, with courage, vulnerability, tears, and a fierce commitment to living. More than anything it happens with love.

When you lose a child, or anyone that you love, it's almost inevitable that you will hear the phase "everything happens for a reason" from at least one person. I don't know if I really agree with that statement. I do believe, however, that we can make meaning out of any experience. Did my daughters die for a reason? Maybe. Quite frankly, I don't care if their deaths were for a reason. I miss them and I love them and they forever changed me. I make meaning out of my experience and out of their lives because that is how I honor them. I choose to make meaning out of their deaths because that is how life feels worthwhile to me.

I, personally, don't believe there's an ultimate plan for my life. I believe that my life is what I make of it. When my children died, I had a choice. I could have given in to the all-consuming grief and pain. I could have given up on life and lost myself in the sorrow of it all. I could have followed through on those thoughts and desires about following them out of this life. For a number of years after Grace's death, that is what I did. I spent years stumbling around in the dark caverns of grief and sorrow, suicide attempts, and living half-alive. I am forever grateful to myself for eventually making another choice.

My life didn't become beautiful again by happenstance. I worked for it. I made the choice to create meaning out of these experiences. I decided that the best way to honor and celebrate the lives of my children was to actually live and experience this life of mine. I clawed my way back out of that cavern of darkness and into the beauty of living again. I let myself feel the grief that I had been trying to shove away. I let myself cry and mourn. I started talking about my children and my love for them. I chose, over and over again, to seek beauty and gratitude in the small, ordinary moments of life. I sought support and guidance from others. I decided what and who I wanted to be out of this experience.

I am a mother.

I am strong.

I am courageous.

I am soft.

I am feisty.

I am resilient.

I am brave.

I am loved.

I am supported.

My children's lives have value. My life has value. My motherhood has value.

So do your children's lives. Living or deceased, your children matter. Your life and motherhood has value, even without your children here. Ask yourself,

What do you want this life to mean now?

I hope that you choose to live fully. That you choose beauty. Choose joy. Choose gratitude. More than anything, whatever the circumstances, I hope you choose love. I believe it is what our children would want for us. I know this is what we all deserve.

Cry and cry again until you can laugh

Mourn and mourn again until you feel alive

Love and love again until you feel full

Get up and get up again until you can stand

Stand and stand again until you can walk

Walk and walk again until you can run

Run and run again until you feel free.

Then be free.

Love.

Honor.

Remember.

Live.

And love them, always.

We are mothers, always.

Dear Invisible Mothers

———————————

Sweet mothers, here is what I want you to know:

You are a beautiful mother. It takes bravery and courage and profound love to mother a child you cannot see or hold or touch.

You are strong. Whether you feel strong or not, you are. Even when you are on your knees in tears. Even when you wish you could have just left this earth with your baby. Even when the best you can do is simply drag yourself out of bed. Even in your darkest moments, you are strong.

It takes strength to mother as we do. To love that which we cannot see or touch is beauty in action. To love beyond death is magnificent.

You are magnificent.

If you are a new or newish mother, know that there is a light beyond this aching darkness. You probably can't see that light yet and you don't have to. I am here holding that light for you. There are many of us here, having lived what you are living. You don't have to know the way. We know it for you.

Just take one step, and then another.

When you can't take a step, it's ok to crawl.

When crawling is too much, it's ok to take a rest.

You will find your way through this darkness of grief and loss and pain.

There is no rush to this journey.

They will be your babies for always. You are a mother for life.

Not even death can take that away.

You love, beautiful mother. You love hard and fierce and deep. This is your greatest gift. Your love will carry you through this deepest sorrow.

Your love will become your light.

Love on, sweet mother, and love always.

xoxo,

Emily

Mothers and Children

Always Together in Love

Caitlin Zinsser and her son, Anderson

Lisa Sissons and her son, Finley Arthur

Paula Gillis and her daughter, Olivia Grace Mathias

Maria LoPiccolo and her son, Bruce Gasca LoPiccolo

Lynn Thumbul and her babies

Amy Whitsel and her son, Brody Micah

Alice B. and her son, Jay B.

Courtney Copeland and her son, Armory Lane

Alenna Barber and her "Little One"

Rachel Bonistalli and her son, Evan Daniel

Rose Marie Vieira and her children, Michael and Christine

Sandy Wedemeier and her children

Jeanie Witcraft-Shaiu and her baby

Veronica Nilsson and her daughter, Nina

Clare Blanchard and her son, Leonardo (Leo) Joseph

Typhaine LeClerc and her son, Paul Benton-LeClerc

Judy Hensley and her daughter, Carol Hensley Singletary

Chrissy Storr and her son, Joel

Renee Bachman and her sons, Stephen and William

Elizabeth Alig and her son, Owen Jude

Analisa Dominica and her children, Ana Lisa and Griffin Daniel

Lisa Krigbaum and her son, Griffin

Sara Tamburrino and her son, Carl Matthew

Tracy Smith and her children, Sammi-Gayle Lynn, Hannah Faye, Christian McKenna, Jacob Richard, Adam Nicholas, Carly Mee

Sandra Norris and her daughter, Naomi Grace

Kaitlin Bevington and her son, Gavin Edward

Heather Thompson and her daughter, MaKenna A. Duff

Kim Openo and her daughter, Logan Grace

Jennifer Johnson and her daughter, Amelia Grace

Lori Davis and her daughter, Elliot Kathryn

Anne Kreber and her baby

Amy Woodbridge and her son, Edward Andrew

Stephanie Seidler and her son, Erryn Shiloh

Audrey Henkel and her daughter, Sofie Olivia

Heather Sue-Dunlap Kimble and her daughter, Hannah Sue Kimble

Rachelle Kamrath and her son, Stanley

And all the mothers who elected to remain anonymous.